TSAR NICHOLAS II
Last Russian Tsar

History Book Age 10
Children's Biography Books

Nicholas II was the last Tsar, or emperor, of Russia. Read on and learn who he was, how he governed, and how he died.

RULERS OF RUSSIA

From 1613 the House of Romanov provided the emperors, or Tsars, of Russia, a huge land stretching from eastern Europe to the Pacific Ocean. The first Romanov ruler, Michael I, was asked to take power in a time of great trouble and unrest. His grandson, Peter I, built up Russia's standing in the world by a combination of wars of expansion and economic reforms.

MICHAEL I

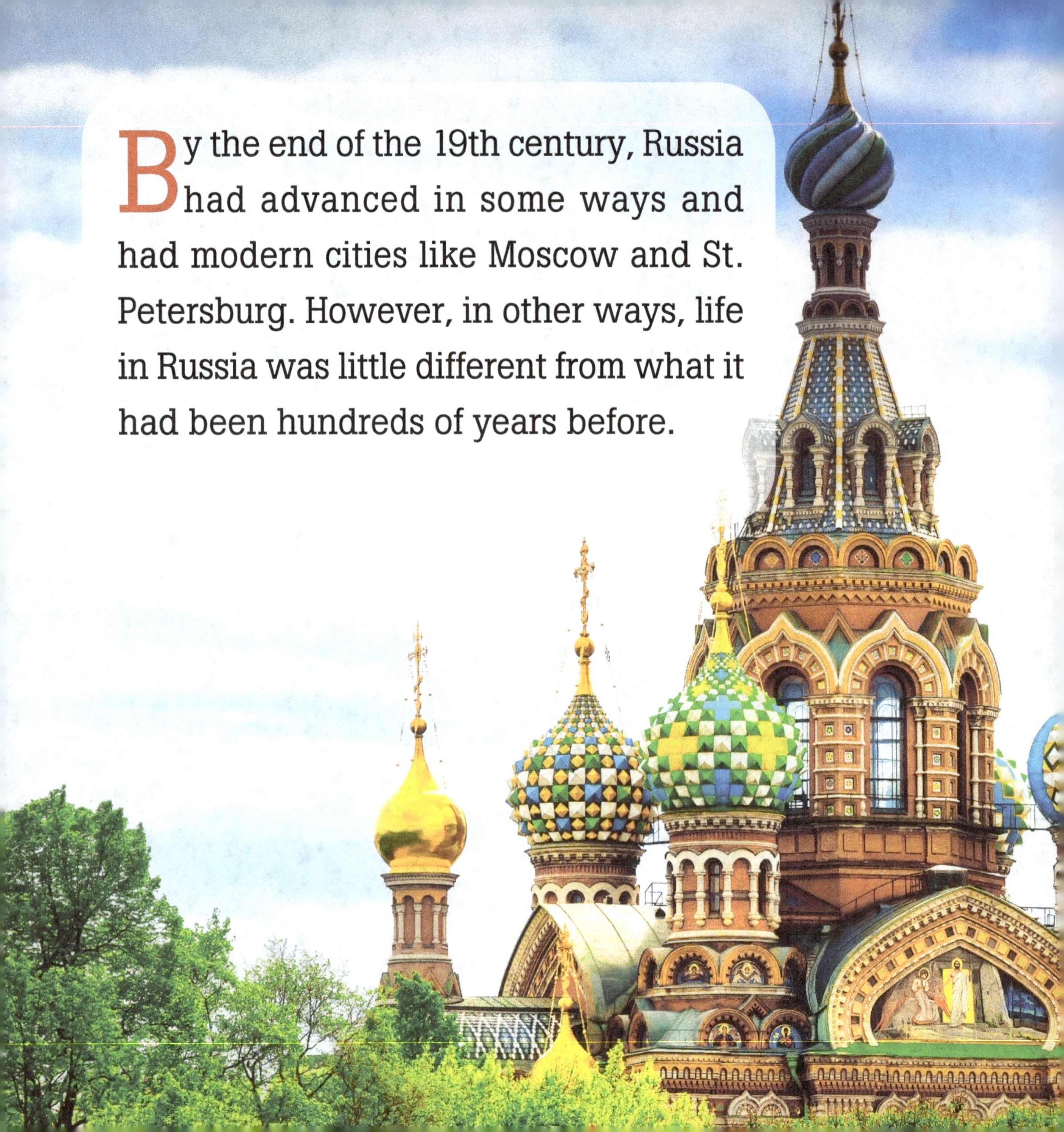

By the end of the 19th century, Russia had advanced in some ways and had modern cities like Moscow and St. Petersburg. However, in other ways, life in Russia was little different from what it had been hundreds of years before.

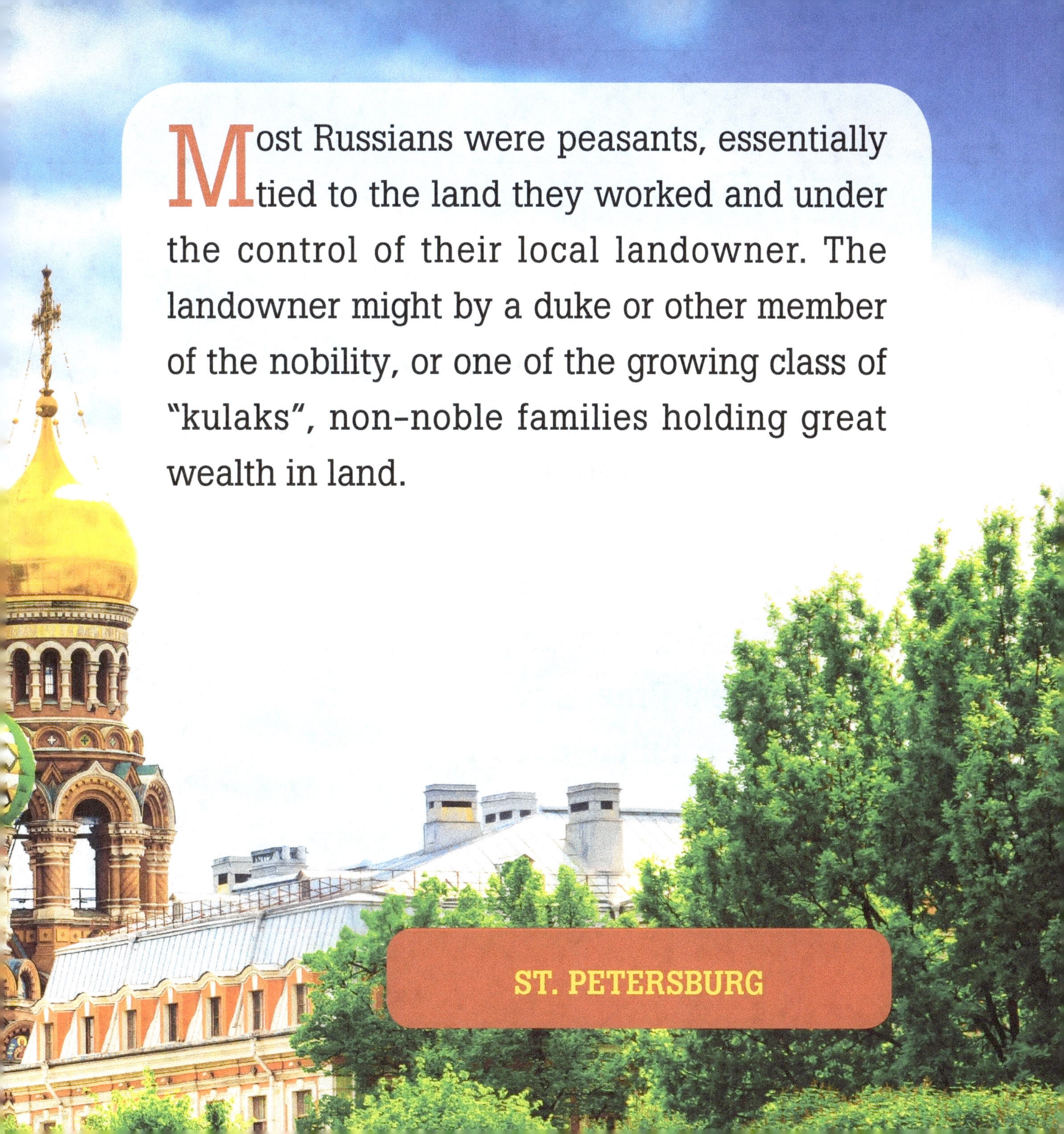

Most Russians were peasants, essentially tied to the land they worked and under the control of their local landowner. The landowner might by a duke or other member of the nobility, or one of the growing class of "kulaks", non-noble families holding great wealth in land.

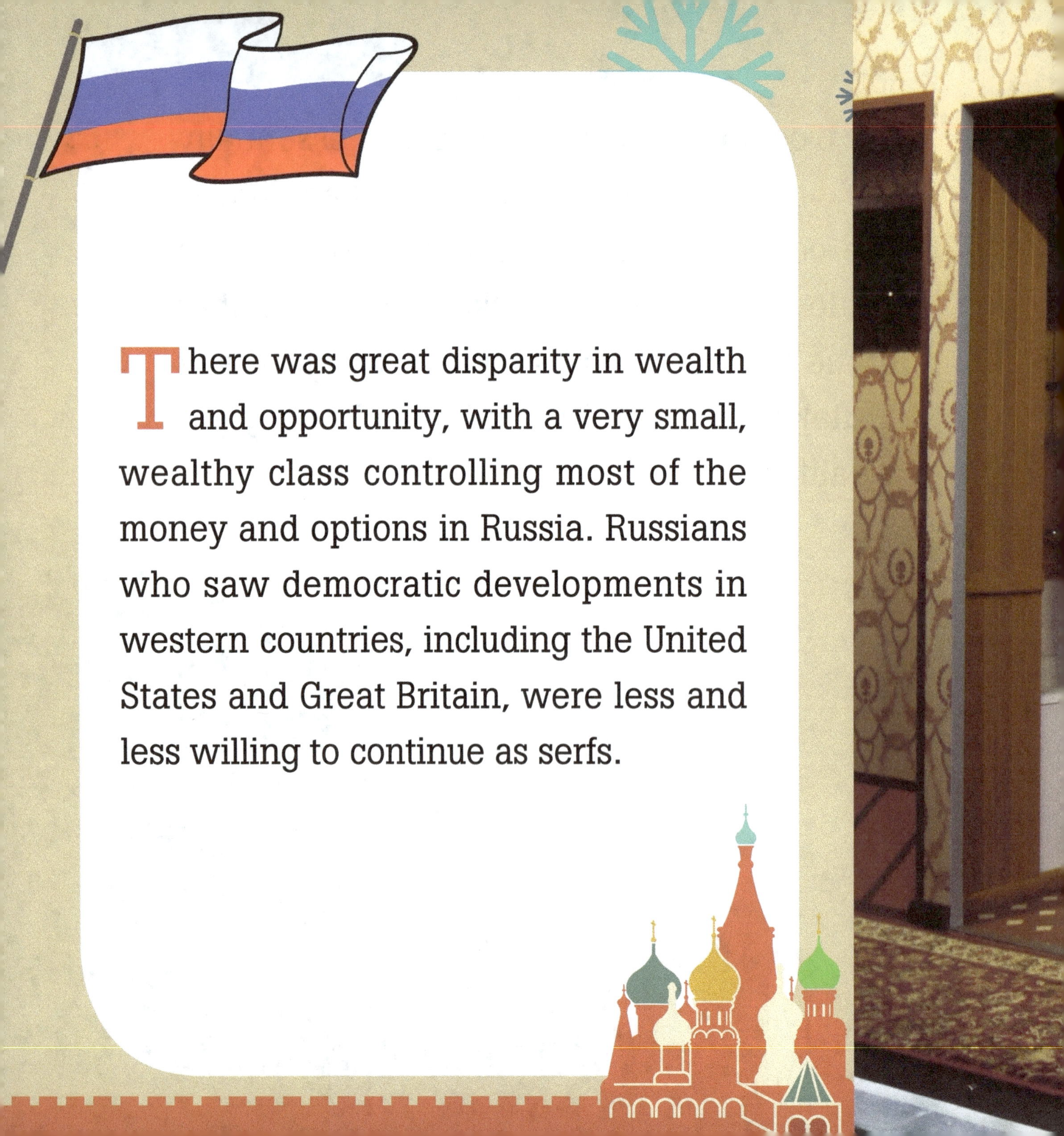

There was great disparity in wealth and opportunity, with a very small, wealthy class controlling most of the money and options in Russia. Russians who saw democratic developments in western countries, including the United States and Great Britain, were less and less willing to continue as serfs.

MODEL OF A 19TH CENTURY RUSSIAN
RAILWAY CARRIAGE INTERIOR

NICHOLAS II OF RUSSIA

NICHOLAS' EARLY LIFE

Nicholas II was born in 1868. His father, Alexander, was the heir to the throne; his grandfather, Alexander II, was the Tsar. His mother was from Denmark. Nicholas grew up in a very conservative household with a deep belief in strong, even oppressive government being the best way to run a country.

Nicholas' education was by tutors. He did very well in history and languages, but did not seem to understand details of politics and economics.

NICHOLAS II OF RUSSIA 1893

In 1881, Alexander II was killed by a bomb, and Nicholas' father became Tsar Alexander III. Nicholas was 13 years old and was now the heir to the throne.

At 19, Nicholas joined the army. He rose to the rank of colonel during three years of active service, but took little interest in political or international affairs.

A CROWN AND A MARRIAGE

Alexander III died of illness in 1894 and Nicholas II became Tsar at the age of 26. He felt completely unprepared for the task of ruling a country. That same year he married Alexandra, a German princess, so he could have a son who would be his successor as Tsar.

TSAR NICHOLAS II OF RUSSIA

CORONATION OF NICHOLAS II

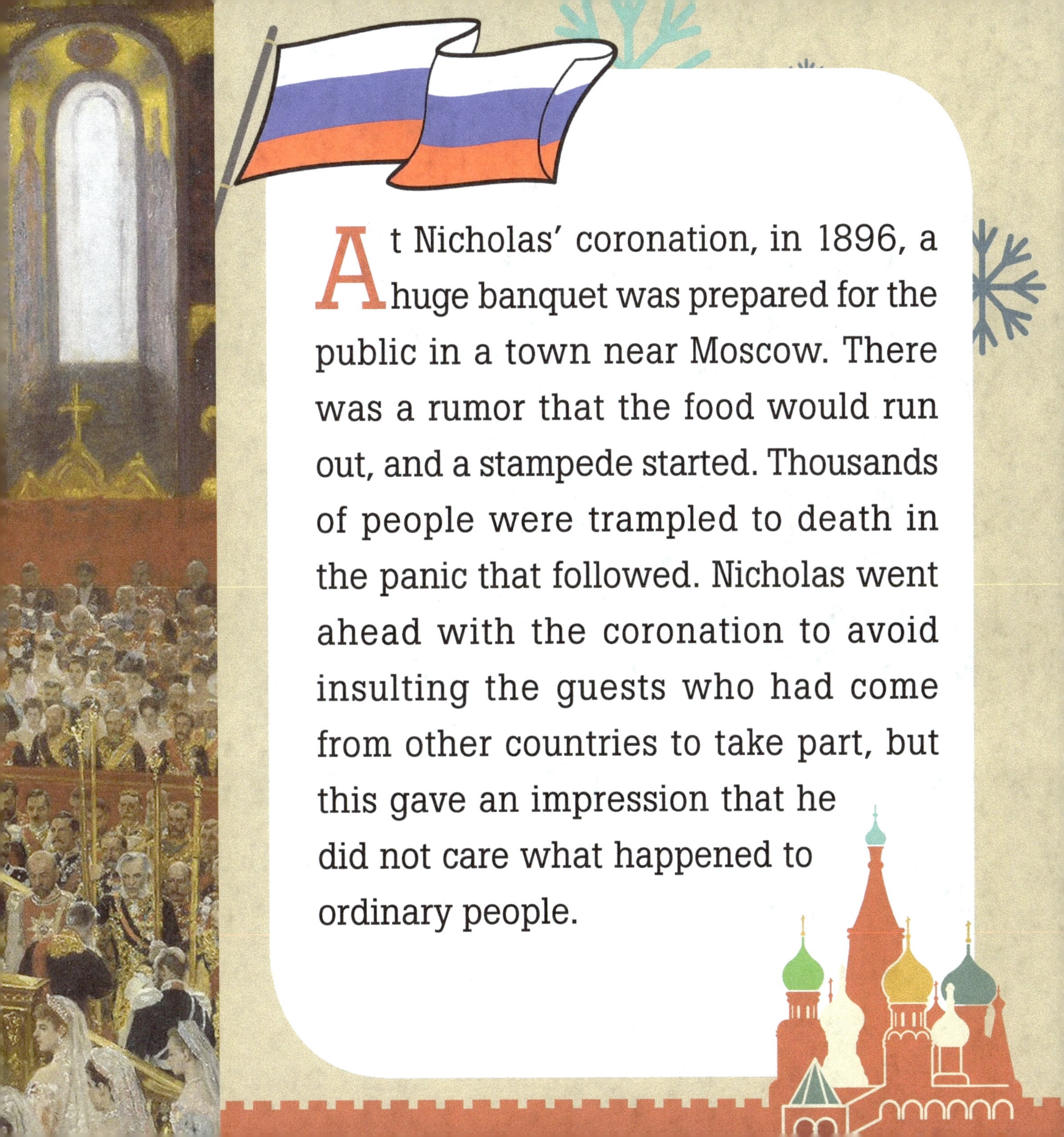

At Nicholas' coronation, in 1896, a huge banquet was prepared for the public in a town near Moscow. There was a rumor that the food would run out, and a stampede started. Thousands of people were trampled to death in the panic that followed. Nicholas went ahead with the coronation to avoid insulting the guests who had come from other countries to take part, but this gave an impression that he did not care what happened to ordinary people.

After four daughters, Nicholas and Alexandra had a son, Alexei, in 1904. The heir to the throne turned out to have hemophilia, a dangerous disease of the blood.

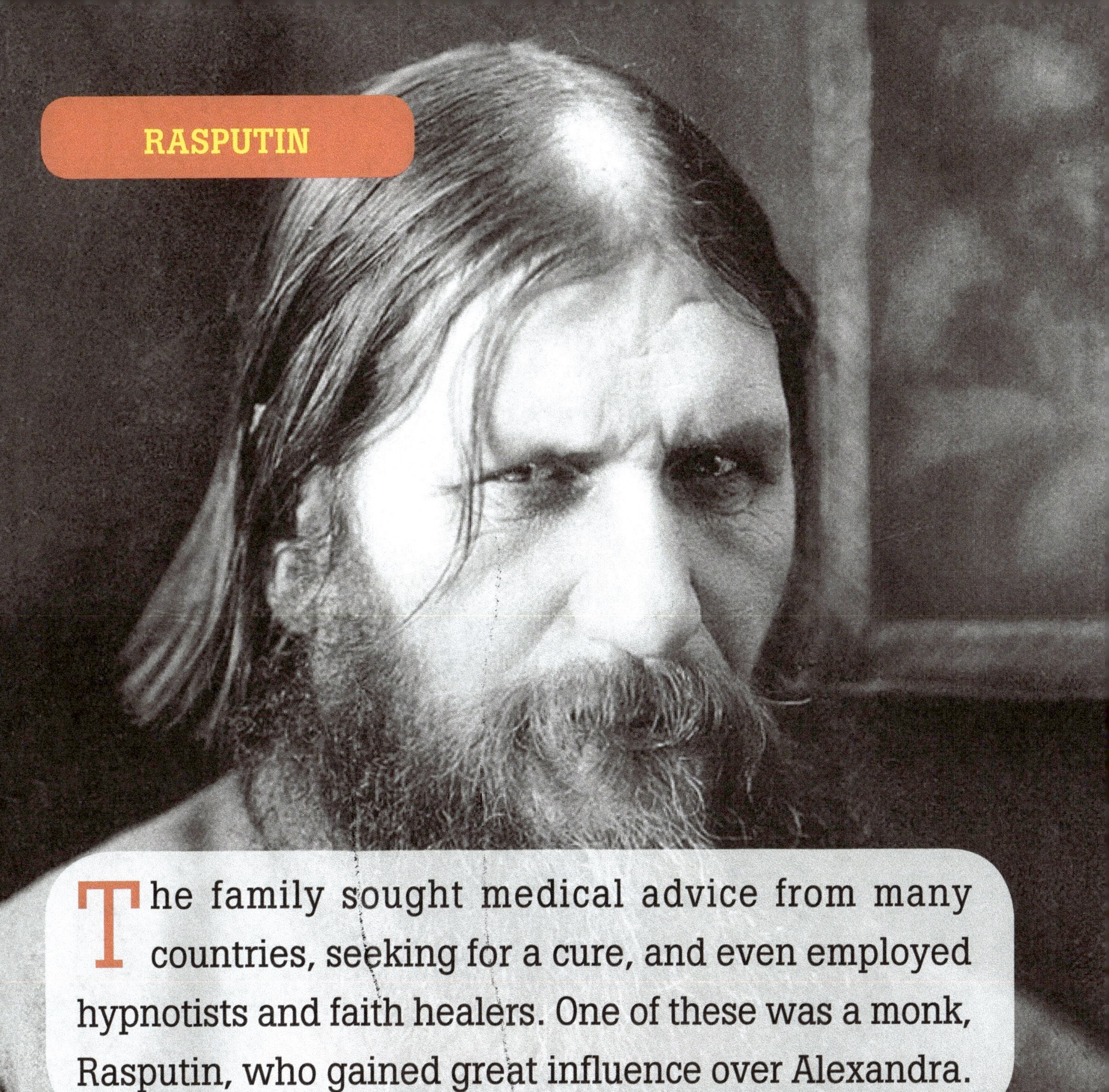

The family sought medical advice from many countries, seeking for a cure, and even employed hypnotists and faith healers. One of these was a monk, Rasputin, who gained great influence over Alexandra.

TSAR NICOLAS II

WARS AND TURMOIL

In his first years as Tsar, Nicholas made efforts to reduce tensions in Europe and to avoid a war there. However, at the same time Russia wanted to expand into Asia. This began to present a threat to Japan, which wanted to expand into the same general area.

In 1904 Japan attacked Russia. Russia was much larger, but much weaker, especially in the far east. Russia lost the war, and lost much of its fleet in a sea battle. It had to give up Port Arthur and other territory to Japan.

PORT ARTHUR

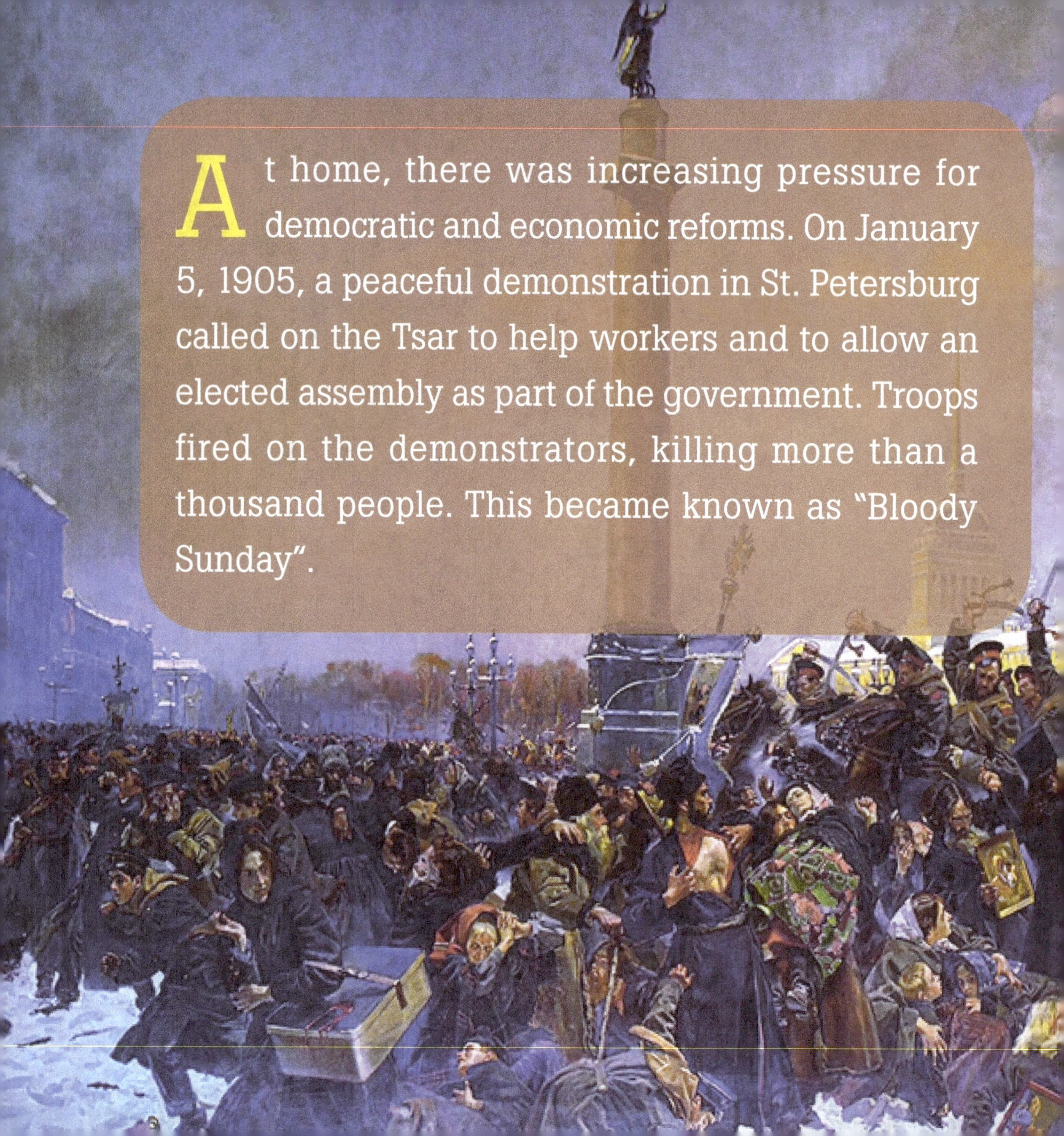

A t home, there was increasing pressure for democratic and economic reforms. On January 5, 1905, a peaceful demonstration in St. Petersburg called on the Tsar to help workers and to allow an elected assembly as part of the government. Troops fired on the demonstrators, killing more than a thousand people. This became known as "Bloody Sunday".

BLOODY SUNDAY

1905 GENERAL STRIKE IN PORI

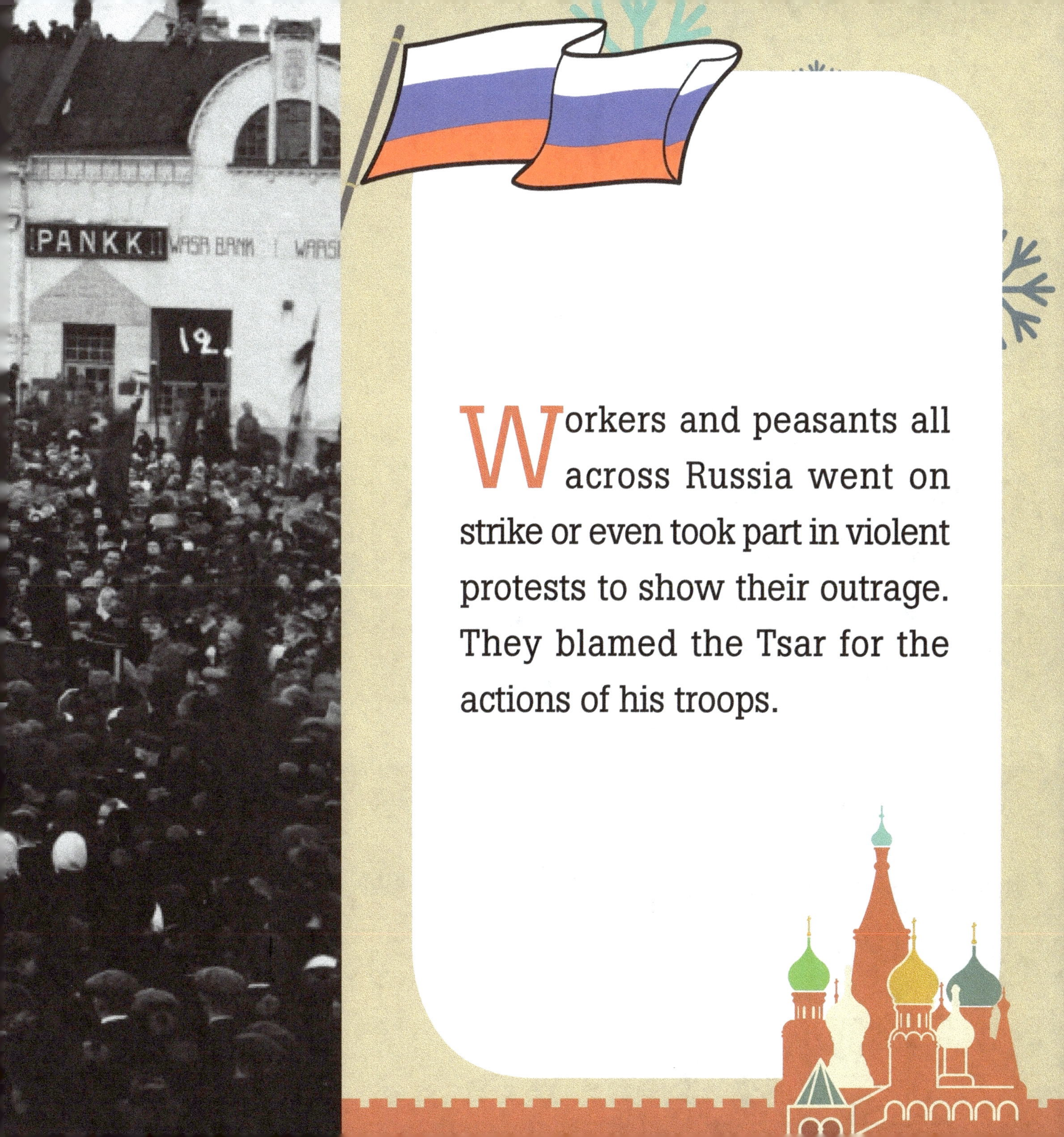

Workers and peasants all across Russia went on strike or even took part in violent protests to show their outrage. They blamed the Tsar for the actions of his troops.

TSAR BOYAR DUMA

Nicholas believed that God had called him to be absolute ruler of the Russian people, but he finally agreed to let an elected assembly be created. This body was called the "Duma". However, Nicholas continued to resist making any real changes to the way the country was governed.

WORLD WAR I

In 1914, tensions between European nations were at a high pitch. A Serbian terrorist killed Archduke Ferdinand of Austria-Hungary. Germany, an ally of Austria-Hungary, demanded that Serbia be punished. Russia, an ally of Serbia, mobilized its army. Germany then declared war on Russia. Other countries joined in on one side or the other, and suddenly a world war had started.

RUSSIAN SOLDIERS DURING WAR I

RUSSIAN TROOPS

Russia's armies did not do well at the start of the war, and Nicholas took over direct control of the military effort. He was a diligent leader, but not a military genius. Also, Russia's army was far weaker than Germany's.

At the same time, Alexandra fell further under the spell of the monk Rasputin. She relayed his advice to Nicholas, who relied on her insights.

This led to many bad decisions. Finally members of the nobility killed Rasputin in 1916, but by then great damage had been done.

ALEXANDRA

THE END OF THE CZAR

Russia endured military defeats, and lost a great deal of territory. Millions of people died, and there was a lack of food because of a shortage of field workers. The public blamed Nicholas for the country's problems, and thought Alexandra had too much influence on the Tsar. Since she was a German princess, many thought she was trying to help Germany win.

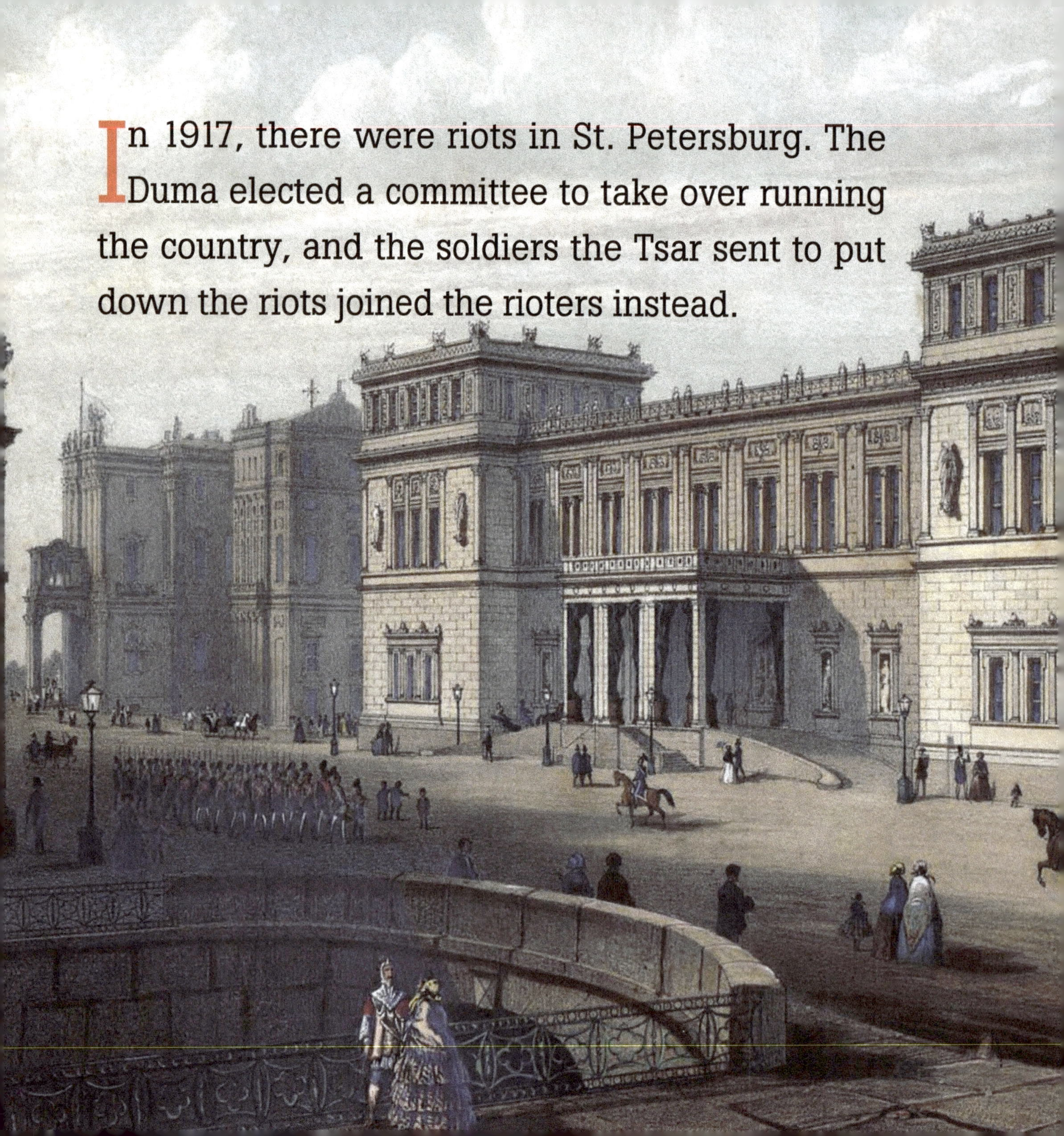

In 1917, there were riots in St. Petersburg. The Duma elected a committee to take over running the country, and the soldiers the Tsar sent to put down the riots joined the rioters instead.

THE NEW HERMITAGE IN ST. PETERSBURG IN THE 19TH CENTURY

RUSSIAN IMPERIAL FAMILY 1913

Faced with a massive lack of confidence and a military crisis, Nicholas felt he had to step down as Tsar. He abdicated (resigned) on March 15, 1917. The new government placed him and his family under arrest and moved them to the Ural Mountains, far from the cities and from the battlefront.

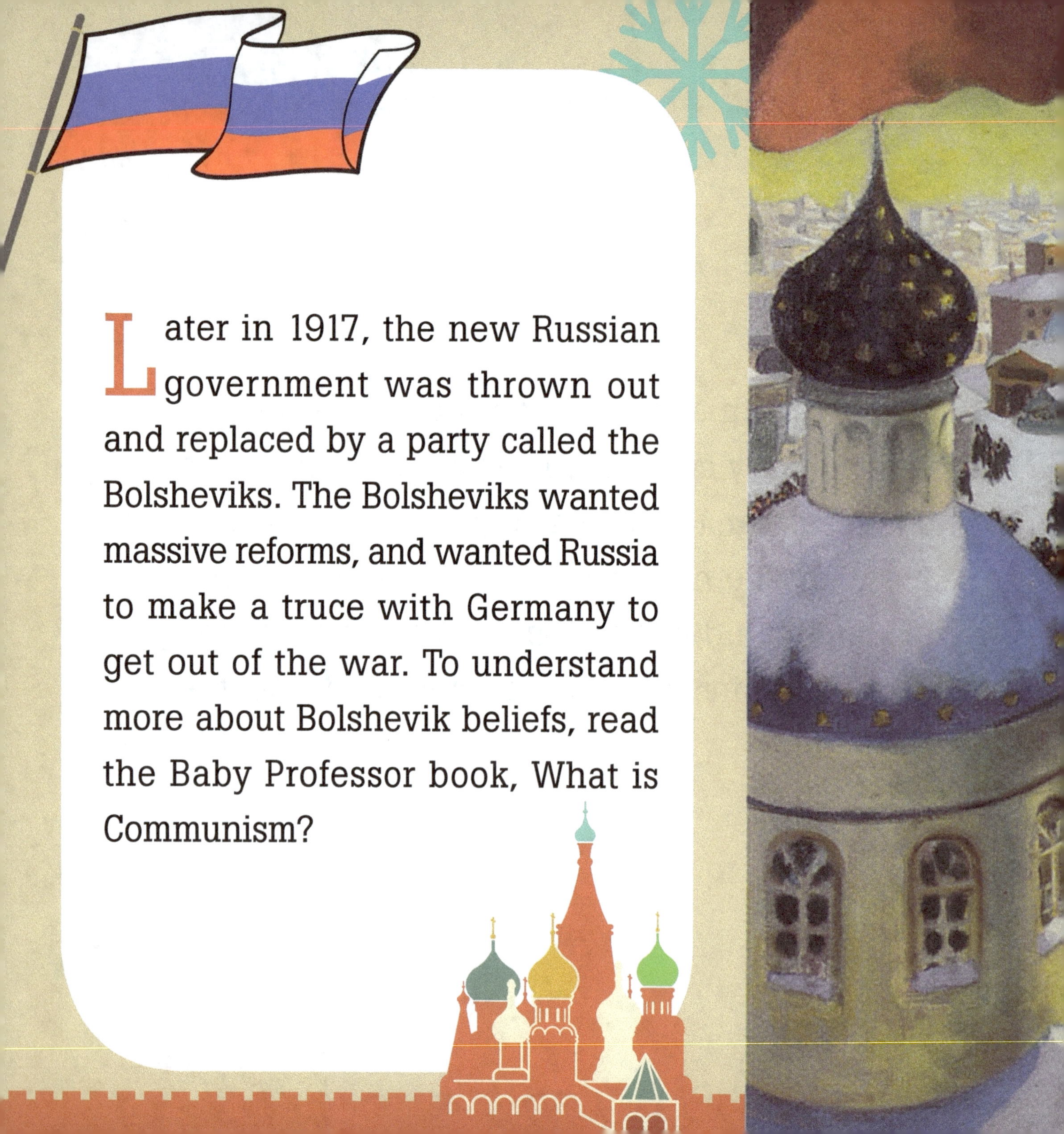

Later in 1917, the new Russian government was thrown out and replaced by a party called the Bolsheviks. The Bolsheviks wanted massive reforms, and wanted Russia to make a truce with Germany to get out of the war. To understand more about Bolshevik beliefs, read the Baby Professor book, What is Communism?

THE RED ARMY BEFORE BEING SENT TO THE CIVIL WAR

By the start of 1918, Russia was in a civil war between the supporters of the Bolshevik government, supporters of the former government, and people who wanted to restore the Tsar to power. The decision was made that the Romanovs were too much of a danger to the Bolsheviks.

I n July, 1918, the Russian government gave orders that Nicholas II, his wife, and their children be executed. They were shot to death in a house in the city of Yekaterinburg.

THE HOUSE WHERE TSAR NICHOLAS II AND FAMILY EXECUTED

THE ROMANOVS 1892

In 1917, there were 65 members of the Romanov royal family. The Bolsheviks killed 18 of them, and the surviving members fled to other countries. There was a rumor for a long time that one of Nicholas' daughters, Anastasia, might have escaped the execution, but DNA analysis in 2007 proved that she was among those who had died in 1918. The Romanov family continues in exile, and several members claim that they should be Tsar, if the Russian royal structure is ever restored. This is not very likely to happen.

CZAR NICHOLAS FACTS

Although things were bad for many people under Nicholas II, they had been much worse. In fact, his grandfather, Alexander II, was called "The Liberator" because of social reforms he brought in.

DELEGATES OF THE FIRST INTERNATIONAL
PEACE CONFERENCE AT THE HAGUE, 1899

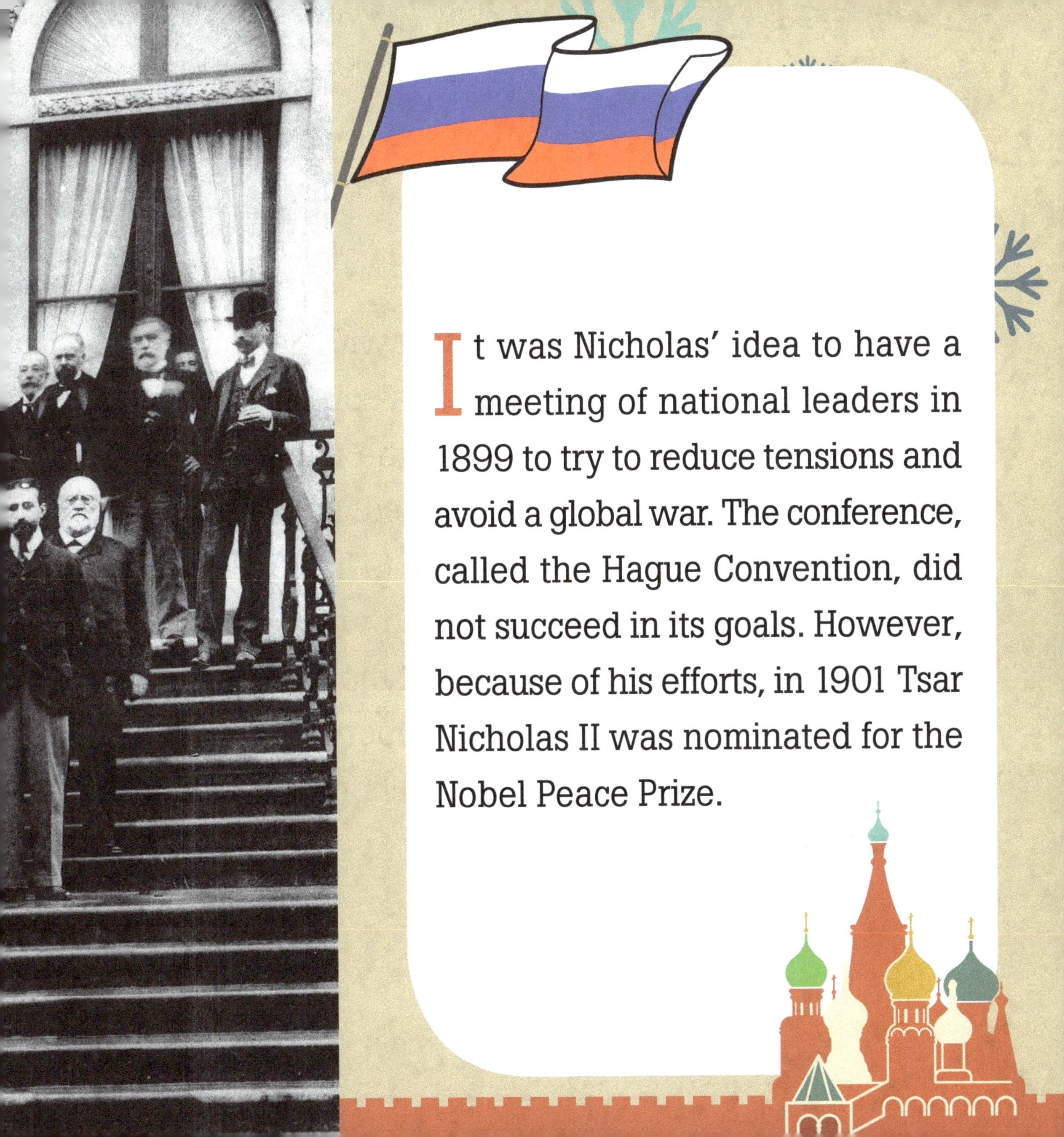

It was Nicholas' idea to have a meeting of national leaders in 1899 to try to reduce tensions and avoid a global war. The conference, called the Hague Convention, did not succeed in its goals. However, because of his efforts, in 1901 Tsar Nicholas II was nominated for the Nobel Peace Prize.

Russia did not have to go to war with Germany, and had little to gain from such a conflict. Although the Russian army numbered in the millions, it was under-equipped and lightly trained. By contrast, the German army had been preparing to fight both Russia and France at the same time, and was possibly the most efficient army in the world at the time. However, Nicholas insisted that Russia support Serbia even if it meant war. More than three million Russians died because of that decision.

BATTLE OF MIŠAR,
SERBIA (1806)

THE RUSSIA STORY

Russia moved from a monarchy to a democracy during World War I, and then very quickly to a new form of government, a "dictatorship of the people". With very brief exceptions, the country has had leaders who have governed very much as the Romanovs did, even though they did not have the title "Tsar".

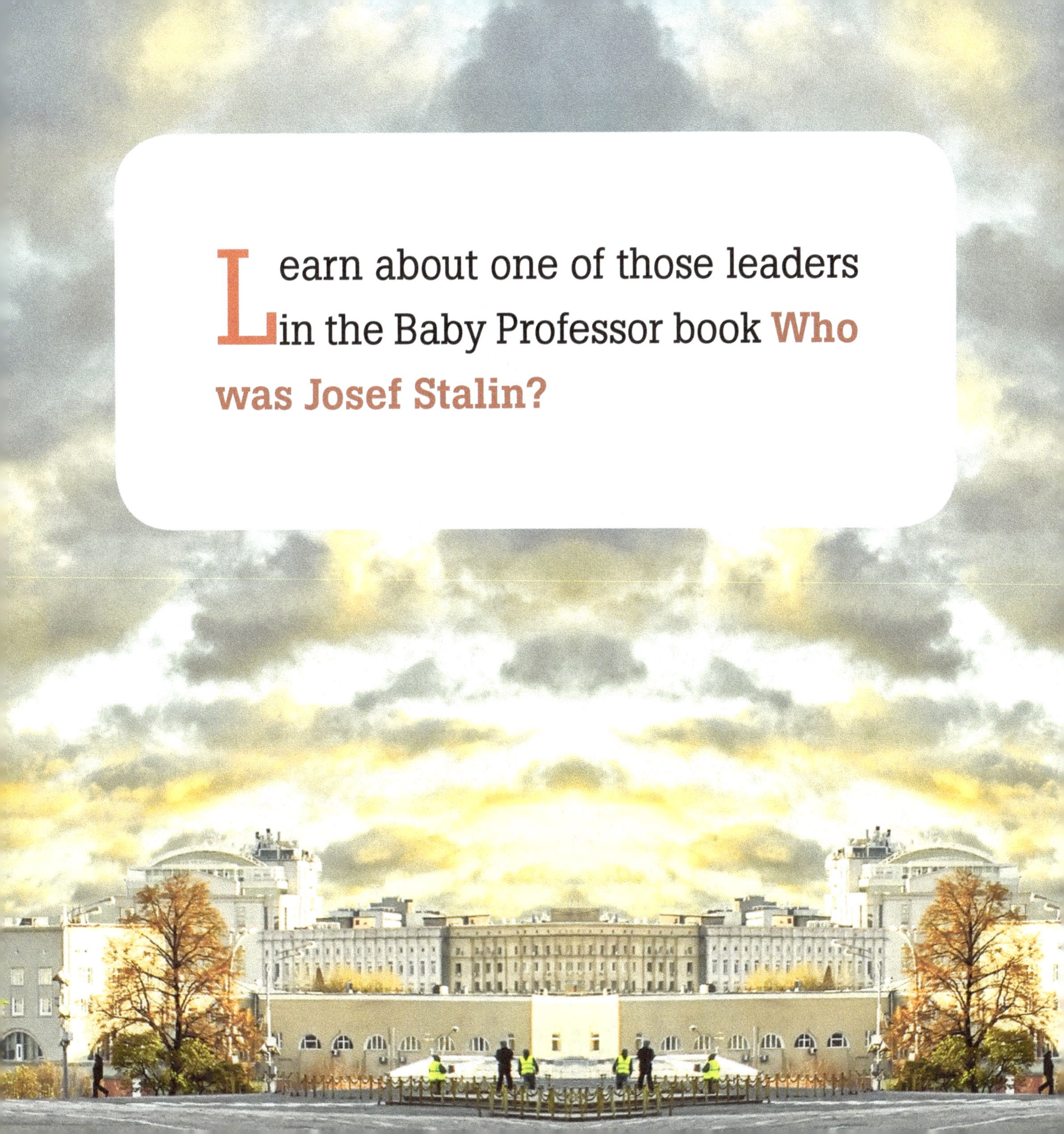

Learn about one of those leaders in the Baby Professor book Who was Josef Stalin?

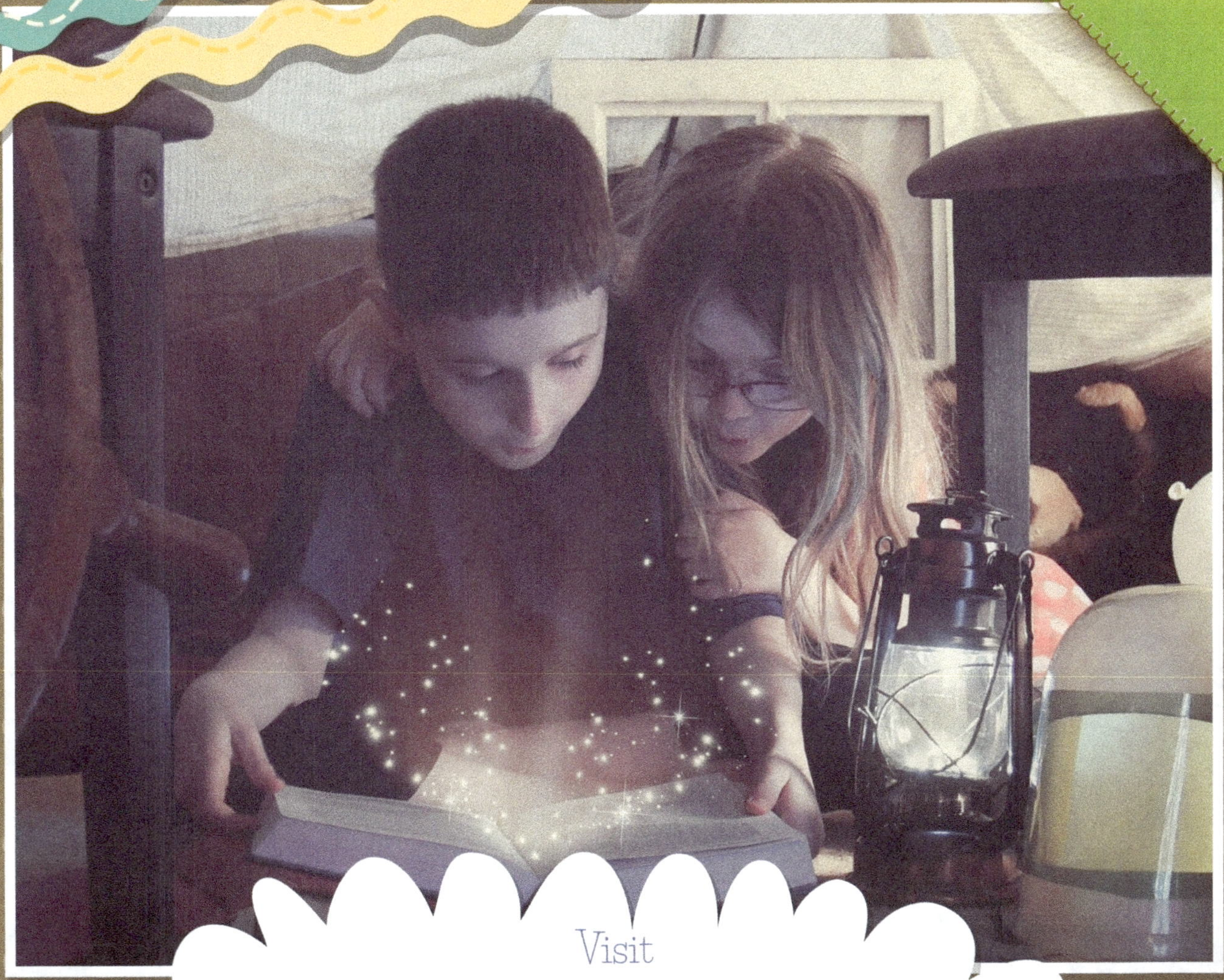

Visit

www.BabyProfessorBooks.com

to download Free Baby Professor eBooks
and view our catalog of new and exciting
Children's Books